The Missing Bone

Louise Spilsbury

OXFORD
UNIVERSITY PRESS

OXFORD
UNIVERSITY PRESS

Great Clarendon Street, Oxford, OX2 6DP, United Kingdom

Oxford University Press is a department of the University of Oxford. It furthers the University's objective of excellence in research, scholarship, and education by publishing worldwide. Oxford is a registered trade mark of Oxford University Press in the UK and in certain other countries

Text © Louise Spilsbury 2016

Illustrations © Richard Watson 2016

Inside cover notes written by Karra McFarlane

The moral rights of the author have been asserted

First published 2016

British Library Cataloguing in Publication Data
Data available

ISBN: 978-0-19-837103-8

10 9 8 7 6 5 4 3 2

Paper used in the production of this book is a natural, recyclable product made from wood grown in sustainable forests. The manufacturing process conforms to the environmental regulations of the country of origin.

Printed in China by Golden Cup

Acknowledgements

Series Editor: Nikki Gamble

The publisher would like to thank the following for permission to reproduce photographs:
Cover&p7t: Dorling Kindersley/UIG/Science Photo library; **back cover, p1** and **p15t&b**: draskovic/istockphoto; **p1tr, p1br, p10** and **p11l**: H. Zell (Own work) [GFDL (http://www.gnu.org/copyleft/fdl.html) or CC BY-SA 3.0 (http://creativecommons.org/licenses/by-sa/3.0)], via Wikimedia Commons (with kind permission from Staatliches Museum für Naturkunde Karlsruhe, Germany); **p1bl** and **p13l**: Martin Shields/Alamy; **p4-8, 10-12, 14l, 16a**: Dave King/Getty Images; **p6l**: Philip Dowell/DK Images/Getty Images; **p6r**: Biophoto Associates/Science Photo Library; **p7b**: Roman Nazarov/Dreamstime; **p8-9**: Lintao Zhang/Getty Images; **p9b**: Design Pics Inc/Alamy; **p11r**: Peter Betts/Shutterstock; **p12**: UCL Grant Museum of Zoology/Fred Langford Edwards; **p13r**: Anup Shah/Nature Picture Library; **p14r**: FLPA/Alamy; **p16b**: Valentina Razumova/123RF; **p16c**: David Marchal/Science Photo Library; **p16d**: Jacopin/BSIP/Science Photo Library; **p16e**: © Xinhua /Alamy; **p16f**: Roger Harris/Science Photo Library; **p16g**: ellobo/123RF

Contents

The Bone

Zac and Jess went to the **museum** at night. They were sleeping there.

"Look, it's a **bone**! We must get it back to the right **skeleton**," said Jess.

Bat Bones

Zac and Jess hunted for the right skeleton.

Fact

Some bones are long and thin. Some are short and fat.

wing bones

bat skeleton

The bones in a bat's wings are light and thin.

"It's not a bat bone!" said Zac.

Panda Bones

"Quick!" said Zac.
"Come up this ladder!"

"It's not a panda bone!" said Jess.

panda skeleton

Bones help animals to stand up.

9

Zebra Bones

10

Jess hit her leg. "Ow!"

Fact

Bones are hard and strong to protect animals from bumps.

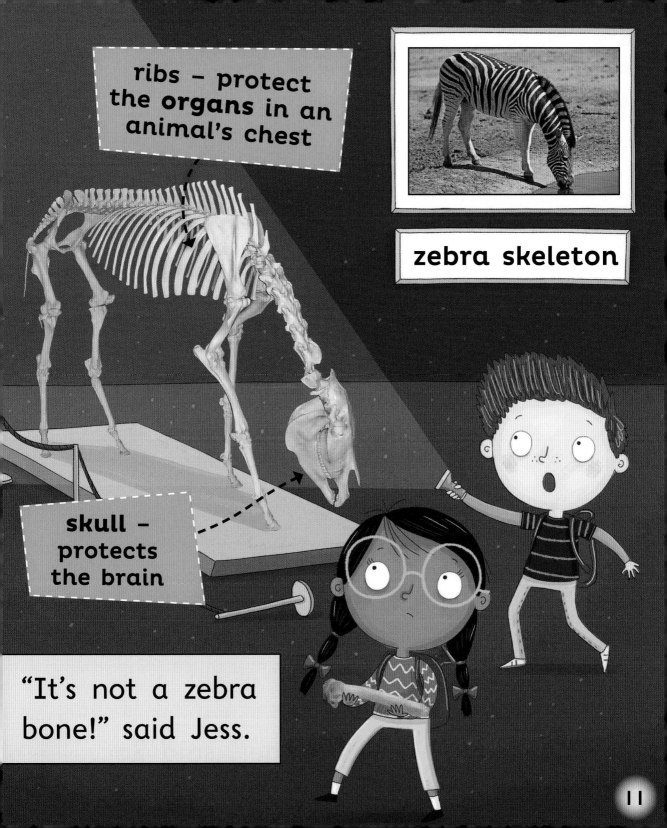

ribs – protect the **organs** in an animal's chest

zebra skeleton

skull – protects the brain

"It's not a zebra bone!" said Jess.

Chimp Bones

"It's not a chimp bone!" said Zac.

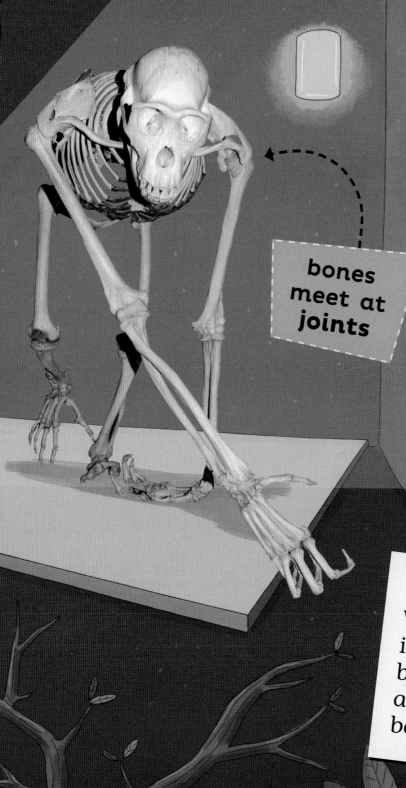

Long arm bones help chimpanzees to swing in trees.

bones meet at joints

chimp skeletons

Fact

When an animal is born it has little bones. When an animal **grows**, its bones grow, too.

kangaroo Bones

Long leg bones help a kangaroo to jump.

kangaroo skeleton

"Look!" said Jess. "The missing bone is a kangaroo bone!"

A Second Bone!

And then Jess and Zac spotted a second missing bone! Can you see the skeleton it belongs to?

Glossary

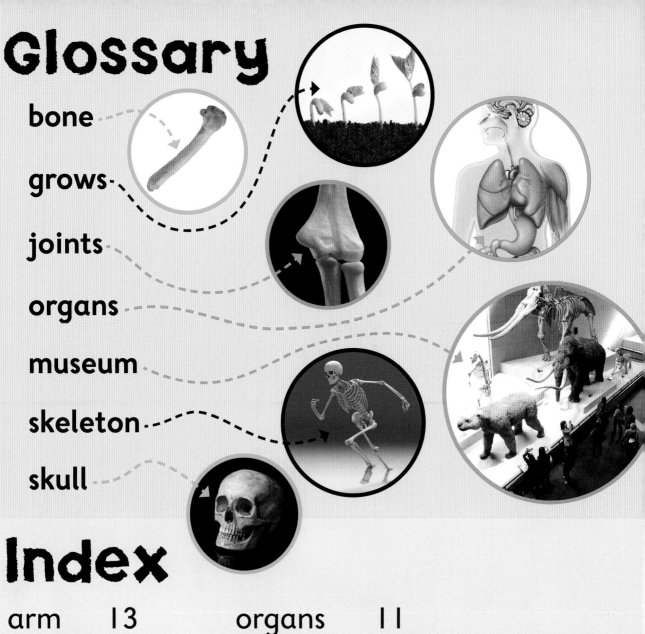

bone

grows

joints

organs

museum

skeleton

skull

Index